I0019742

NETWORKING WITH FACEBOOK

A GUIDE FOR NON-NATIVE ENGLISH SPEAKERS

DOROTHY ZEMACH

WAYZGOOSE PRESS

CONTENTS

INTRODUCTION: USING FACEBOOK IN ENGLISH

As of 2018, Facebook had 2.23 billion active users every month. That's more people than live in any country on earth! Facebook is available in 101 languages, everything from Arabic to Zulu, including Corsican and Maltese.

However, the most common language on Facebook is English. If you have a friend who lives in Corsica, it's likely you'll communicate on Facebook in English, rather than Corsican. Your friend, of course, will communicate in English with some people, and in Corsican with others.

So what language should you use on Facebook?

There is no one answer for everybody. Naturally, you will use your native language, and connect with others who speak that language. But what you want to connect to someone who doesn't speak your language—that friend in Corsica, for instance—you might want a bilingual Facebook presence, in both your language and English. You could post a status update first in your native language and then in English—that way, everybody (or almost everybody!) would be able to read it. Or you might post about some topics in one language, and other topics in a different language.

However, if you never post *anything* in English, do not be surprised if people who only speak English do not accept your friend requests. It doesn't mean they don't like you! It just means that they can't read anything on your page, so there doesn't seem to be a good reason to connect.

You already know that different countries, and indeed different languages, have different cultures and customs. It's the same on Facebook. There is a certain 'culture' of communicating on social media platforms in English. The purpose of this book is to help you use Facebook successfully in English, to fulfill your goals and form strong and positive relationships with other people.

People, in any language, have different personalities. It is not possible to describe only one way to communicate or to use a platform such as Facebook. There will always be exceptions. The goal of this book is to help you get along with most people in most situations, when you are using Facebook in English. But you will, of course, have to use your own common sense, good judgment, and kind heart to communicate successfully with others.

———

A note on language: English, like all languages, is constantly changing. I believe in a decade or so, the pronouns "they" and "their" will be commonly accepted in a singular sense, even in written language (as they now are in spoken language). This book, then, uses "they" to refer to one person, who could be any gender.

CHAPTER 1

GETTING STARTED

Let's get ready by looking at your existing Facebook account and making some plans. First, here are some questions to ask yourself.

WHAT IS MY GOAL?

What do you want from Facebook? Even if you think this is a very basic question, take the time to answer it. Write your answer down, even. (That will force you to put it into words). For example,

- Do you want to reconnect with friends you've lost touch with?
- Do you want to share ideas and discuss issues with other people who do the same sort of work you do, or who have the same hobby?
- Are you looking for work or opportunities to study or travel?

- Do you want to publicize events or programs you're involved with?

WHO WOULD I LIKE TO CONNECT TO?

I don't mean specific people; I mean, what *kind* of person?

- Someone who has the same job? Someone who lives in the same community?
- Someone who lives in a country that interests?
- Someone who likes the same music or games?

WHAT DOES MY FACEBOOK PAGE LOOK LIKE NOW?

Log out of Facebook, and then visit your page as if you were someone else. What impression do you think a stranger would get? (Can they get an impression at all, or is your account very private?) Do you think your page is meeting your goals? Why or why not?

Now, log back in and check a few things.

1. Are you happy with your **profile picture**—is it clear and current? Is your **background banner** attractive? Does it show something meaningful to you? (Note that some people do not like to accept friend requests from strangers if their profile photo is not of their face.)
2. Go back through all the **photos** that you have posted, and that other people have posted and tagged you in. Do you want them to be visible to the world? Are there any you'd like to delete?

3. Check the **pages** you have liked. Are you still interested in those things? (Remember—other people can see everything you have liked.) If there are any you're no longer interested in, remove the like.

4. Check the **groups** you have joined. Are you still interested in all of them? (As with page likes, other people can also see which groups you belong to, if they're public.) Leave any groups that no longer meet your needs and goals. If there are groups you still want to belong to, but right now, you don't want to see all the posts in them, visit the group and turn off notifications. You can still remain a member.

5. Check your **friends** list. You can *unfriend* anyone you don't wish to be connected to at all, of course. You can also *unfollow* someone (permanently, or just for a little while) if you want to remain friends, but not see their posts. If you unfollow someone, they can still see what you post. People considering your friend request might check to see who your current friends are.

6. Finally, check your **privacy** settings. How much do you want to show the world? If you make everything private, then other people will not be as likely to accept your friend requests (because they won't be able to see anything about you and your behavior). If you give too much information, you could be at risk for things like identity theft. For example, I have my birth month and day posted, because I enjoy having friends wish me happy birthday. But I don't have the correct year of my birth—that gives too much information to identity thieves, and my friends aren't interested in it anyway.

A note about privacy: You should be aware that many of your actions on Facebook intrude on your privacy in some way. Every time you click on an advertisement or follow a link or play a game or answer a "fun" survey, you are giving away information about yourself. That isn't necessarily dangerous or bad, but it does make you more vulnerable. In any case, you should be aware that it is happening, and make a deliberate choice to participate (or not!).

It's a good idea to not post words or images on Facebook (or any website) that would damage you if they became public. Facebook does have some privacy controls, but as we know from reading the news, privacy controls can fail, and hackers can be very clever. Protect yourself by simply not putting very sensitive information online—ever.

———

OK! Now that your Facebook account looks and performs how you would like it to (or, well, mostly—sometimes Facebook annoys us all, no matter what we do!), it's time to explore networking.

CHAPTER 2

MAKING NEW FRIENDS

HOW FACEBOOK WORKS

You might think Facebook is pretty simple: you open an account, you upload a photo, you connect to some friends, and then you post your thoughts—and then your friends all read what you wrote.

Actually, it's not that simple, not that last part. All of your friends will *not* see what you wrote. Not because they didn't log on or because they didn't pay attention, but because Facebook doesn't show all your posts to all of your connections.

In the same way, you will not see all the posts your friends write—because Facebook won't show them to you! Facebook chooses *some* posts to show you. There is no easy way to get around this; it's just the way Facebook works. However, there are some ways to see more posts from certain people.

If you do any of these things when you see a friend's post,

then Facebook will show you more posts from that person in the future:

- 'Like' or choose a reaction
- Write a comment
- Share the post

That is one reason why some people write things like "If you agree, like and share this!" They are trying to make their post more visible to other people. The more popular a post seems to be, the more people Facebook will show it to.

If you realize that you haven't seen any posts from a certain friend in a while, go to that person's page directly, and like or comment on a few posts. Then you will see more posts from that person in the future.

It works in the other direction too, of course—the more interaction there is with one of your posts, the more visible that post—and you—will become.

Certain types of posts that you create will be more visible—for example, posts that include an image. If you ask a question or introduce a topic that encourages people to respond, that will increase visibility. Chapter 3 will give you more ideas about what to post.

CHOOSING FRIENDS

Who should you connect to? If you are using Facebook to network, then you want to connect to people who are interesting, informative, and inspiring. You might also wish to connect to someone who is well known in your field.

If you are considering sending someone a friend request, click on their account and read a few screens of posts. Are they interesting? Are they the kind of posts you want to read regularly?

Remember, however, that sometimes you cannot see all of someone's posts—or even any of them—depending on their privacy settings. After you send a friend request and are accepted, you might see more.

It is tempting to connect to as many people as you can—but I don't advise this. If you connect to someone who isn't really interesting or relevant to you, then that person's uninteresting posts will fill your newsfeed, and crowd out other people whose posts you would rather see. You don't get more points in life if you have more friends. The only value that connections have is value that they contribute.

CONNECTING TO STRANGERS

Do you want to connect to someone you don't already know? Take a moment to imagine what they will think about your request.

Many people will accept friend requests from people they don't know—but not everybody will.

When I receive a friend request from a stranger, I visit their page and ask myself, "What do we have in common?"

- If the person is an English teacher or a writer or an editor, like me, I know what our professional connection is.
- Facebook will tell you if you have any friends in

common. If we have 65 friends in common, and all of those friends are connected to teaching English, then I can guess why the person wants to be my friend.

- If, on the other hand, we have only one friend in common, I assume that Facebook has "suggested" me as someone to connect to, but we might not actually share any interests.

If we have nothing in common, I don't usually accept the request.

If we have something in common, I next check the person's page to see if they post interesting things (see Chapter 3). If the page is boring, then I don't refuse the request—but I also don't accept it. The person stays forever in the "request" position. Then they can't send me another request.

If you want to connect to someone, and you don't think the other person will immediately understand why, it's polite to send a quick PM (personal message) to explain, like this:

> Hello, I'm a Spanish teacher at the high school level. I read some of your posts in the discussion group for Spanish teachers and was impressed with your understanding of intermediate learners. If it's OK, I'd like to connect on Facebook to continue those conversations.

> Hi, I'm interested in connecting with you on Facebook. I see we have several friends in common, including X and Y, and I'm also an electrical engineer. In fact, I'm attending the national conference for engineers in July, and noticed that you are giving a presentation. I am too.

However, be aware that Facebook often sends messages from people who are not already connected as friends to a special "requests" folder, and the other person might not notice your message right away. So be patient.

RECEIVING FRIEND REQUESTS

It can feel strange or intimidating to receive a friend request from someone you don't know. Should you accept? Will they feel insulted if you don't? Remember—your Facebook page is yours. You only want to fill it with people who will add something positive to your life.

You don't have to make a decision immediately. Wait until you have some free time, and then visit that person's page.

- Check their personal data—is it filled out?
- Do you have some idea what they do and where they live?
- Do you have any friends in common?
- Check the pages they've liked and the groups they've joined. Do you have a lot in common?
- Can you figure out why they chose you as a potential friend?

If you don't want to accept the request, you can either decline it or do nothing. If you (they will only know that you have not yet accepted it). If you accept a friend request and later realize it was a bad decision, don't worry—you can unfriend that person, and even *block* them. (A person who is blocked will not be able to see anything you post or to send you another friend request.)

CHAPTER 3

POSTING

Some posts work well; some don't. In this chapter, we'll be exploring why.

A post that "works well" is one that people read and respond to, perhaps with a "like" or a comment. It's a post that makes people think, or gives them some information, or amuses them, or makes them think well of you, or encourages them to take an action.

Think back to your goals. What are you hoping to do?

- Discuss issues and ideas?
- Entertain?
- Inform people about ideas that are important to you?

Keep your goals in mind as you choose what to post. Also, your posts will (and should!) reflect your own personality. It's hard to say that certain types of posts are always great or always terrible. But these guidelines will help you think about the effects your posts will have on others.

POSTS THAT (USUALLY!) WORK WELL

Want to increase interaction on your page and create a positive impression? Try some of these types of posts.

Personal stories that entertain or inform

Your friends are connected to you because they are interested in you (we hope!). So information about **you** is usually more interesting than the state of the economy.

- Did you take a nice hike last weekend?
- Did your child graduate from high school?
- Did you have some painful dental work?
- Did your best friend share a great recipe for chicken?
- Did your refrigerator stop working, even though you only bought it two months ago?

Short 'stories' about incidents like these let your friends know what's going on in your life, and what you think about it. People also know how to respond—*Wow, that lake looks lovely!* or *Oh, I hate dental work! But at least your teeth are healthy now.*

I've found that funny personal stories are more popular than anything else.

For example, I wrote once about walking to work, wearing a pair of jeans, and after a few blocks, I felt something slip down my leg… and in a few steps, it fell out onto the sidewalk. It was a pair of underwear that I'd worn the last time I wore those jeans. (Fortunately, I scooped up the underwear before anybody noticed!)

It's not an important or special story; it's just a funny thing that happened to me, and that made me feel a bit foolish. But people loved that story. They laughed, they made some jokes, they shared embarrassing things that had happened to them.

Topics of general interest or important news

Sometimes, though, it is important to talk about the state of the economy. But you want to get a discussion going, it's still important to present things in a way that encourages a reaction. Consider these different possibilities:

- *The economy sucks! Everybody is poor.* **X**
- *I admit I'm worried about the economy and the future. My daughter is starting university next year, and asked me what she should study to ensure she will have a good job in four years. I don't know what to tell her! Any suggestions?* √
- [link to article about the economy] **X**
- *I just read this in my favorite news magazine, but I'm not sure I agree. It says that cutting taxes is the best way to grow the economy. But then won't the city have less money to make improvements? I'd be interested to hear my friends' ideas.* [link to article about the economy] √

Questions

A question invites a response—so when you ask a question, people can interact because they can answer. Even phrasing a thought as a question instead of a statement can bring more interaction. Look at the difference:

- *I hate it when the phone rings when I'm taking a shower.*
- *Is there anything worse than when the phone rings and you're in the shower?*

They say the same thing, but the first one is more likely to get just likes, and the second one is more likely to get people answering *I know! I hate that!* or *Sometimes I think my phone only rings when I'm in the shower. Should I take more showers?*

People also like being helpful. So asking a genuine question lets people offer you their advice. Ask questions like these, and people will post their suggestions:

- *What are some good books in English that I can buy for my son? He's 12, and reads at a high intermediate level.*
- *Help! I spilled coffee on a white blouse. How can I get the stain out?*
- *Are there any MS Word experts out there? I'm trying to copy one document into another, and every time I do that, I lose the tracked changes.*

Related to this is the practice of **crowdsourcing**—asking a crowd of people (your friends on Facebook) for their ideas. You might see posts like this:

> *I'm crowdsourcing for an article I'm writing on time management. What's your favorite method for battling procrastination?*

If you want to see an example of someone using questions well on Facebook, check out science fiction and fantasy author Daniel Arenson (whose first language is not English). Notice not only the questions he posts, but how many people answer. Now that's a lively page! Some recent questions:

- *Do horror movies legitimately scare you? Or are they just good fun?*
- *Is there such a thing as good and evil? If so, how do you define them?*
- *What is your ultimate comfort food?*

https://www.facebook.com/Daniel.Arenson.Books

(And yes, you are welcome to follow Daniel and answer his questions too, even if you have not read his books.)

Memes

In Internet language, a *meme* is an image that is widely known online, accompanied by some text (which changes frequently). They are very popular on Facebook. Some common memes involve famous actors or animals in humorous poses.

Follow the same guidelines for posting memes that you do for posting links. Ask yourself

- Have too many other people already shared this image?
- Does it communicate something that is important or amusing to me?
- Will my friends understand why I posted it?

I've noticed that I get better responses when I post memes

that are funny. They are even more popular than memes that are profound or inspiring.

You can make your own memes by choosing a favorite proverb or saying (or your own original idea) and adding it to a photo. Free and copyright-free images can be found on

http://www.pixabay.com.

If you don't already have a program that adds text to images, you can use

http://www.canva.com

(which has some free and some paid features, but adding text to your own images is free).

You can easily add text to popular meme images at

http://www.makeameme.org

or

http://imgaflip.com

Not all memes are successful, however. Many have poor English (incorrect spelling, grammar, or punctuation) or aren't accurate.

For example, I found this meme on Facebook once. Can you tell what is wrong with it?

Blessed are the
hearts that can bend;
they shall never
be broken.

Albert Camus

Does this one give you a hint?

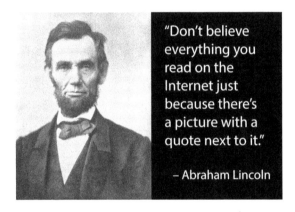

"Don't believe
everything you
read on the
Internet just
because there's
a picture with a
quote next to it."

– Abraham Lincoln

I was suspicious about the first one because I have read novels by Camus. While the sentiment in the meme was nice, it didn't sound like something Albert Camus would say.

It isn't always easy to tell if a quote is accurate. Unfortunately, googling the quotation isn't always enough to give you the answer. If you google "Blessed are the hearts that can bend;

they shall never be broken," you will see many, many sites that attribute it to Albert Camus. But they are wrong.

According to a wonderful site called Quote Investigator https://quoteinvestigator.com/, this thought was first expressed by Saint Francis de Sales. It was later chosen and translated in 1829 by a man named John Peter Camus. Probably someone attributed it once only to "Camus," and the Internet decided that it must have been the more famous Camus—Albert.

Don't spread false information (or bad English) by sharing poorly created memes. Do a little detective work on quotations before accepting them. In addition to using Quote Investigator, you can check some popular mistakes about quotes here:

https://en.wikiquote.org/wiki/List_of_misquotations

And remember, you can easily redo a meme yourself to make a better version, if necessary.

Remember too that if you are sharing a meme, it is highly likely that at least some of your friends have already seen it. The first time, or even the second time, that you see something, it might seem funny or profound. The 20th time, it's only tiring.

However, the Internet has a short memory, so if you really like a meme that is making the rounds, save it to your computer. Then wait a few months before posting it, so it will feel fresh again.

Photos

If you go somewhere interesting or notice something that's beautiful or funny or makes you think, take a photo and post it to Facebook with a short comment. (An image with no comment will get less attention!) You don't have to be a professional photographer; you just have to choose pictures that have some meaning, express something, or show something that's important to you.

Photos of other people

You've had a wonderful lunch with your friends, and the server took a photo of everyone on your phone, and now you'd like to post it on Facebook. Should you?

The answer is "It depends"—it depends on how your friends would feel. The polite thing to do is ask them. Even if you feel everyone looks great in the photo, they might not agree. Perhaps someone is shy, or feels they didn't look very good, or they just don't like having photos of themselves online. Show the photo to everyone in it, and ask if it's OK to post on Facebook. I usually say yes when people ask me, but I always, always like to be asked.

Here's an example of a time I said no when someone asked if they could post a photo.

I was living in a country where alcohol was forbidden to citizens of that country. As an American, I could purchase alcohol through the US Embassy store, and drink it indoors with other Americans. At one such event, someone took a photo; and I asked that it not be shared on Facebook. To me, it felt disrespectful of the country I was in. Someone else might not mind at all, of course. But the point is, I did mind, and I didn't want the photo posted. And so the person didn't post it.

If the people say yes, however, then go ahead and post the photo. It's a nice way to commemorate the occasion and celebrate your friendships.

Links

If you have discovered an interesting or important news story that you think people should know about it, you can post the link on Facebook by copying and pasting the url. It's very common for people to share links to news stories or events or websites.

However, links can be annoying (or boring) if you post too many of them, especially if you just post them without any commentary. There is a strong chance that if you are posting links with no commentary, your friends are not clicking on them. So instead of being helpful or interesting, you are only wasting their time—and yours.

When you post a link, then, write a few sentences about it. Did something surprise you? Do you agree or disagree with the opinion? Why do you think the link is important to share? Where did you find it, and why did you choose it? Write something, in other words, that makes it personal. Here are some examples:

- *An article about a new type of bicycle developed in Sweden. Do you think it would ever catch on here in Los Angeles?*
- *I heard this song on the radio and it reminded me of my*

parents. They played this song at their wedding. I still think it's one of the most romantic songs I know.

- *I think this proposal to cut funding to public education is a terrible idea. Make sure you vote on November 20!*
- *According to this article, most of us don't get enough sleep. I have some of the symptoms they described. Do you? How can I get more sleep?*

Be aware of how many other people are posting the same link or news story, however. If all of your friends are sharing the same thing, that means many people will open their news-feeds and find the same article coming up again and again. So before you share a link, ask yourself if it is something that will be new to your friends.

You can also post a link to a song you like on YouTube; but again, explain why it's meaningful to you.

POSTS THAT DON'T WORK WELL

Remember that most people have not come to Facebook for a lecture. They want to interact. That is, they want to chat and discuss. Therefore, your most successful posts will usually be ones that people can react to—that they can comment on or add something to.

Selfies

What is there to say about someone else's selfie? Well, not much. Someone can say, "You look great!", but it feels strange to say that again and again and again. It can feel like the other person is 'fishing for a compliment' (asking for praise). Too many selfies can seem like bragging or showing off.

Fishing for a Facebook compliment

That doesn't mean you should never post a selfie. But decide for yourself how many selfies is reasonable—one per month? five per year? only ones in some interesting location? only ones with other friends?

Don't just think about how much you like taking and posting selfies—think (honestly) about what you expect and want your friends to say. Are you hoping they will tell you that you look attractive? Are you showing off some interesting place you have visited? How will other people feel looking at your photos?

Vague-booking

This is a term given to posts that don't really explain what the person is referring to, and therefore don't give any information. Often vague-bookers are trying to force their friends to ask them questions.

For example, a person might vague-book a remark like

Nothing hurts more than the betrayal of a friend. You think you can trust some people, but then you get a terrible surprise.

But what does this really mean? Has the poster been betrayed by a friend? If so, who? and how? Or is it just a general commentary on the notion of betrayal—and if so, why is the person posting it? There is no way to know unless you comment and ask: *Gosh, Helen, is everything OK?* But although people do like to support their friends, most people do not like being manipulated into asking questions. After some time, vague-bookers might notice that their friends respond less and less often.

In short, if you want to say something, then say it. If you are not comfortable truly sharing a thought or experience, then don't—but don't just leave a few vague hints.

Photos that aren't your own

When I seen a photo of something like a sunrise or a park, I might comment *That's lovely. Where is it?* But sometimes I'll get an answer like *I don't know. It's not my photo. I just found it.* Oh. Well, then I'm not very interested... What can I say? *Wow, you are good at finding things with google?*

It's different, though, if the person posts a photo and makes a personal comment—for example:

I found this photo of a beautiful sunrise, and it made me feel peaceful and hopeful at the same time. Even though sunsets are beautiful, I think I like sunrises even more.

Now there's something personal, and a reason for the photo—
and people will be more likely to respond.

Posts that are too angry

People do love to read complaints, especially if they are
common ones. But if you have clearly lost your temper, you
can seem irrational, unreasonable, or even dangerous.

Consider the difference:

- Argh! I'm so frustrated with my Internet company! I
  pay $60 every month, and it's still so slow. And last
  night—again—I lost access for over three hours. They
  should refund some money every time I have no
  access. √
- I hate Company Q. They are nothing but liars and
  thieves. They should be killed. **X**

Remember: what you post on Facebook lives on forever, somewhere—certainly in people's minds. It's best not to post when
you are upset. Calm down first and then decide if you want to
write about it at all.

Content Facebooks considers inappropriate

Facebook will often remove posts that contain sexually
explicit images, hate speech, or profane language, although
not always. They are more likely to remove posts if someone
complains about them (and you will not be told if someone
complains, or who that person was).

But even if Facebook does not remove a post that might seem offensive, your connections will see it, and they'll remember and form an opinion about you. Think carefully (as always) about your audience, your goals, and the impression you are trying to make.

————

A Note about Politics and Religion

Online communication is no different from communication in person in this regard—these are topics about which people not only disagree but have very strong feelings. We naturally tend to become close friends with people who share similar views, but it's possible to have a wide range of acquaintances —as well as work colleagues and family members—whose beliefs are very different.

Your Facebook page is your own, of course, and you are free to express your views. But you should be aware of how your friends will react. You should also be prepared for how *you* might feel when someone disagrees with you. Are you OK with that? Or will you decide to block that person? What if it's a family member? What will you do if two of your friends have an argument with each other—on your page?

There is no one answer about what you should do with your own page. You will have to make your own decisions. However, you should be much, much more careful about posting your political or religious beliefs on other people's pages. Even if you know what your friend believes, you might not know what your friend's friends believe.

I know people who use Facebook intensively for networking

or marketing who have a strict "no politics ever" policy for themselves. They still have opinions, and discuss those with friends and acquaintances; just not on Facebook.

Because I have friends from so many different religious backgrounds, I actually delete any kind of religious post or comment that someone else puts on my page—even if it's something that is meant to be kind, like *Merry Christmas* or *Happy Ramadan*. (That doesn't have to be your policy—I'm just telling you mine.) It's not that I disapprove if someone else celebrates Easter or Hanukkah or some other religious festival! But I feel the place to announce that sort of thing is on their page, and not mine.

There is no right or wrong answer or one way to behave; but it is an issue you should think about, so you are posting with consideration.

BEHAVIORS THAT ANNOY OTHER PEOPLE

Although different people like different things, almost everybody I've ever spoken with agrees that these things are annoying:

- Adding someone to a group without asking them first
- Sending personal messages to someone you don't know well
- Sending personal messages to a large group of people (so when one person responds, everybody gets that response)
- Tagging many people in one post (so when one person responds, everyone gets a notification)

- Posting a photo of someone without their permission (especially if it's not a flattering photo)
- Selling something or advertising something too often
- Inviting people to play a game—especially if you do it more than once—without asking first if they want the invitation
- Inviting people to an event that they couldn't possibly attend (because they live in another place)
- Asking people to "like" your page—especially if you do it more than once
- Posting too many details too often, especially boring ones (*Woke up at 7:00, then had breakfast. Here's a photo!* or *Driving to work now* or *I think I might go to bed early tonight.*)
- Bragging too much (Some is fine! It's only "too much" that's a problem.)
- Complaining too much (Some is fine! It's only "too much" that's a problem.)
- Responding to a post without reading it carefully (and therefore misunderstanding it)
- Not reading other people's responses first (in case the answer you want to give has already been given by someone else).

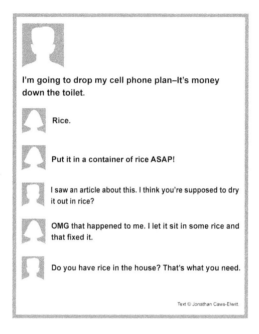

Remember to read posts carefully before you respond!

FAQS (FREQUENTLY ASKED QUESTIONS)

How often should I post?

Not too often, and not too seldom. I know that's not very precise! Yet it is the real answer.

Twelve times a day is too many; you're not giving other people space to talk, and it can feel overwhelming. "Like trying to drink water from a fire hydrant," as they say.

But once every three months isn't often enough—your posts won't get shown to many of your friends, because no one has interacted with you recently.

Once a day or once every a few days is probably about right, although you will need to experiment a bit and see what works best for you and your friends.

———

What should I write/do on other people's pages?

There's no one answer to this question, because it depends on the other people. You need to be observant and sensitive. Do your friends ask questions? Then by all means, answer them. If they post a photo or a story, then they are probably hoping you will offer a comment or reaction.

Be careful about posting information directly on someone else's page. It can feel intrusive. I don't recommend that unless you know the person well, and are very sure they would welcome your post. Don't ever post anything that could seem like personal advertising (*Buy my book!* or *Like my company page!* or *I'm having a sale at my store!* or *I'm giving a webinar!*). The place for announcements like that is on your own page.

If you have a photo of your friend, instead of just posting it yourself on their page, consider emailing it or sending it by PM, so your friend can decide whether or not to post it.

———

What language should I post in?

Great question! Who are you trying to connect with? Post so that those people can read something on your page. If you speak several languages, and different friends speak different ones, then it's fine to post in more than one language. You could make a bilingual post (Spanish on top, English on the bottom). You could post local news in Arabic and questions about English language teaching in English—and so on. Always think about your audience.

———

When should I "poke" someone?

Never.

But what if I...

No, never.

What about...

Really. Never. Just don't do it.

———

When should I use the "wave" function on Messenger?

See "When should I poke someone?"

———

What should I do if someone upsets me?

Disagreements happen on Facebook, just as they do in face-to-face communication. One advantage you have online, though, is the ability to walk away, wait some time, and then think before you respond.

Sometimes the best choice is to simply ignore the upsetting comment. You don't have to respond to everything just because it exists. You don't even have to answer a question just because someone asks one.

Remember, though, that your page is your page. If you really feel upset by a comment on your own page, then I suggest deleting it. You have that power. If the person then posts another upsetting thing, unfriend them. If necessary, block them. Your Facebook page should be a positive space for you.

———

What should I do if someone I'm connected to isn't very interesting, but I still want to stay friends?

This is what "unfollow" is for. If you unfollow someone:

1. You will remain friends,
2. they can still see what you post, and
3. they will never know.

CHAPTER 4

GROUPS

People interested in the same topic interact in a Facebook group. There are groups to discuss everything from astrophysics to zoos. There are groups for sports, hobbies, music, cities, schools, politics—you name it!

Facebook has three different types of groups:

- public (open)
- closed
- secret

Public groups are visible to everyone. If you searched on Facebook for "organic gardening," for example, in the "Groups" section, you would see hundreds of listenings. Some of those will be open—meaning that anybody can join just by clicking "join."

Anybody can see that a public group exists, read the posts, and view the members. Only members can add posts and comments, though.

Public groups tend to be large; they can have thousands or even tens of thousands of members. Therefore they tend to be more general and to go off-topic more often. They're also more likely to be bothered by spammers and advertisers.

————

Closed groups still show up in searches, but only members can read posts and see other members. After you join, you'll be able to see everything. To join a closed group, you'll click "Join group," just as you would for a public group, but then you'll have to wait for a group administrator to approve you. Sometimes there is a simple question to answer; this helps the administrator avoid automated advertisers and bots.

Closed groups are usually smaller than public groups, though some can still be quite large. They're generally more focused, probably as a result of being smaller.

If you post something in a closed group, it is not easily available for non-group members to see (in theory, it's not visible at all—but you should still avoid saying anything you wish to keep completely confidential. In a large group of people you don't know, there's a chance that someone would share what you wrote without asking).

————

Secret groups do not show up in searches, and are not shown on anyone's profile. If you check my profile (which is public), you will not see any of the secret groups I belong to. The only way to join a secret group is to be added or invited by the owner of the group—or to start one yourself! Note that you need to be a friend of the group administrator in order to be invited or added, which is not true of public or closed groups.

Secret groups are usually much smaller, and often all of the people in the group know another; they all know the group owners, of course, because they couldn't have joined otherwise.

In small, secret groups, your posts are more private, and there is less chance someone will share your information without permission. However, it is still possible for someone to take a screenshot or copy and paste something. The only 100% reliable way to keep information on Facebook from being shared is not to post it at all.

POSTING IN GROUPS

In any group, someone begins a discussion by posting something (called *starting a thread*); then, other people add their comments. Just as on a personal page, you can type a comment in response to the first post, or as a response to someone else's comment.

If someone changes the topic with their comment, this is called *hijacking the thread*, and is usually considered poor manners. If you want to talk about a different topic, then start a new thread.

The same conventions for personal pages apply to groups—that is, the most popular threads are those that invite discussion. A link that's posted together with commentary or a question will get more engagement than a link alone.

Comments that add opinions or ask questions will also stimulate more conversation than ones that just say something like "Thanks for sharing."

Many groups will even post rules—about what kinds of topics are allowed or policies against sharing information, for instance.

If you are using Facebook with a certain goal in mind, such as finding a job or moving to a new area or meeting a certain kind of person, groups will probably be more useful to you than your personal page—especially closed and secret groups.

LANGUAGE

Because groups will generally have members who are not friends of yours, it's usually best to keep language polite, friendly, and even a little formal. In very small groups, you might be more casual, of course; but as always, think carefully about your audience.

People who text and post line sometimes use abbreviations and shorthand in English, such as *u* for *you* and *ur* for *your*. They might not capitalize the first word of a sentence, the pronoun *I*, or proper nouns. They might skip punctuation inside sentences such as commas and quotation marks, or end punctuation such as periods.

I do not advise using this kind of language in large groups, though. While it can be faster to write this way, the results are harder to read. (For most people, anyway!) But when you are posting for other people to read, you want your message to be clear and easy. To save yourself time but cost someone else time is not polite.

Consider the difference in tone:

- What time is your webinar?
- wut time is ur webinar

Abbreviations and shorthand can also seem slangy and very casual. Sometimes people deliberately try for that effect; perhaps they belong to a circle of friends that considers those words cool or fashionable.

There aren't any 'rules' about language on Facebook, so I will just say again: think about your audience, your purpose, and the impression you are trying to make.

DEALING WITH PROBLEMS

Typical annoying behaviors in groups include

- posting too much
- going off topic
- posting incorrect information
- disagreements, bullying, or harassment

Posting too much

No matter how small or how large a group is, some people just do more of the talking. They might be more knowledge-able about topic, have more time to devote to the group, have been with the group longer... or they might just like to hear themselves talk (or write)!

If you are the person who set up the group, you can message your over-talkers and say things like

- *You seem very comfortable with social media, Ana. Could you help me encourage some of the other members?*
- *I want to try something for a week: you and I will only post questions, but not our own answers or any comments. Let's see if that works! We'll discuss it next Thursday.*

If you are not the person who set up the group, it's harder to influence other people's behaviors. But if you have serious concerns, you can send a private message to a group administrator, and perhaps that person can help.

Going off topic

Sometimes lively discussions go off track—that is, someone responds but changes the topic of the original post, or thread. A little of that is normal and not a problem. But changing the topic too much can be confusing. Here are some sentences you can use if this happens, with the key phrases underlined:

- *So, to get back to our discussion of ways to save water…*
- *That's an interesting point. Could you make a new thread about that?*
- *Let's not hijack Luiz's thread. Let's stick to talking about the entrance fee, OK?*

Posting incorrect information

What should you do if someone posts information that isn't true? Well, first, of course, you want to be sure that it is the other person who is wrong, and not you. Do your detective work before you publicly disagree!

Then, if you want to correct the misinformation, you can

- Ask questions: *Are you sure that was Albert Camus? It doesn't sound like him. Do you have a link?*
- Politely disagree or explain: *Actually, I think it was a different Camus who said that. Check this link: …*
- Message them privately to let them know they made a mistake (note that this will only work if it was a genuine mistake, and not a different opinion)

Disagreements, bullying, or harassment

Even in small, secret groups, misunderstandings can happen; or you might just disagree! It's easy for some kinds of people to lose their tempers online and post things that are angry or unkind. People can say something as a joke that is not understood by other members, who take it as an insult. Writing is communication, but you don't have the benefit of other cues such as tone of voice and facial expressions to help show what you are really feeling.

If someone writes something that upsets you, it's best to wait a little before you answer. See if you can understand why the person wrote what they did. If you don't agree with someone's opinion, that's OK—you can 'agree to disagree,' as the saying goes, and still remain polite.

Remember that it's not easy to change someone's mind ever,

and certainly not on Facebook. You can explain your ideas once, maybe twice; but then it's probably best to let it go. The other person does not 'win' if they write a comment after yours. You just have different opinions, and that's OK.

If someone truly upsets you, however, you can block them. Then you will not see anything they post, and they will not see anything you post. This is a pretty extreme measure, but it's there if you need it.

There are even people who deliberately try to upset other people just to get a reaction. This kind of person is called a *troll*, and the behavior is called *trolling*. Trolls enjoy provoking other people, so the more you react, the more they will increase their trolling behavior. The best way to stop a troll is to not respond at all. If this is too hard to do, then block them! You can also report trolling to the group administrator, who may choose to remove the troll from the group.

PAGES

Businesses on Facebook can create pages. They're not quite a group, and not quite a personal account. A business page is a place for announcements. Sometimes business pages are set so that visitors cannot post directly on the page, although visitors can usually comment on posts that the page owner makes.

If you have a business, consider making a page for it. Be sure to fill out all of the information sections (such as what you do, your hours, your website address, and so on), so your customers can find you!

If you 'like' a business page, it's important to remember that Facebook won't necessarily show you all of the posts from that page. Be sure to visit the page directly from time to time. The more you interact with a post (like it, comment on it, or share it), the more posts you will be shown in the future.

CHAPTER 5

MESSENGER

Messenger, Facebook's direct messaging system, has its own special benefits and annoyances.

A PM (personal message) sent through Messenger is felt immediately. You get a notification instantly, and often in several places—on your computer and on your phone, for instance, perhaps with a buzz or a ding or a vibration. It feels important and urgent. Therefore, if someone messages me, I expect it to be important and urgent.

Examples of instant messages that seem justified:

- *Hey, did you sign that contract? Remember, it's due by 5:00 pm today.*
- *Mom, can you call me? I have a question about our joint bank account.*
- *I'm on my way to the airport, but I just ran into bad traffic, and might be 15 minutes late to pick you up. Please wait by the information booth and I'll be there as soon as I can.*

- *The seminar room just got changed! It's now in room 304, on the third floor, by the main stairs. See you there!*

Examples of instant messages that do not seem justified:

- *hi*
- *how are you*
- *what's up?*
- *hello my dear how r u*
- *where are u from?*

I get a lot of messages like those in the second group. A **lot** of them. They do not feel polite or friendly. They feel like harassment. They're an intrusion into my very busy day. I cannot spend a few hours every day writing *fine thanks and u?* to 1,736 people. It is not useful, practical, or even possible.

Perhaps in some cultures, messages like these are common and welcome. You might be sending such messages with the very best of intentions. However, in English, intrusions like these, especially those from men to women, feel either romantic or somewhat threatening. It is simply not the custom in English for strangers to send private messages for no reason. If you want to have a conversation with someone you don't know well, interact on their main page, in public. Don't send a private message.

Remember: Facebook is not just about you. It's about the other person too. When I get a message like this: *I want to practice my English with you okay?* the person isn't offering me anything. Instead, that person is asking me to do my job (teaching English) for free, for a stranger. Would you go to the garage of a mechanic you had never met, open the door and say "Hi! Fix my car now! Thanks dear!" and expect the mechanic to abandon their other scheduled customers and immediately attend to your car... and then not get paid?

If you find yourself getting too many messages from strangers that say only things like *hi how are you doing*, I recommend pasting in a response like this one:

> Thanks for your message! I only use Messenger for family members. All other communication takes place on my main page, in public. Thank you for your understanding!
>
> **Note**: This is an automated message service, and it is unmonitored. The sender will not see any reply.

Then, if you still get a reply after that, ignore it. Do not respond, no matter what! If the sender continues to send you messages, then you can block them. It is possible to block someone on Messenger but still stay connected to them as a friend on Facebook. This is also a useful option for someone that you still want to be connected to, but who sends you too many group messages and chain letters and videos and things on Messenger.

Even worse than the instant message is the surprise phone call. It's true that the telephone function on Messenger can be very, very useful—a way to make free phone calls! However, I only want to receive a call from someone I know, and from someone I'm actually expecting a call from.

Recently I had the unpleasant experience of being called by a Facebook friend: another English teacher, but not someone I had ever met in person. However, he lived on the other side of the world. So when he called, the phone call woke me up—at

3:00 am. I thought it was an emergency—perhaps an ill or injured family member. When I saw it was a stranger from Facebook, I was furious, and refused the call. I sent the person a message the next day asking him to never call me. I received no apology; but a month or so later, he called again. Again in the middle of the night. And so, I blocked him.

The one time that it is OK to send a PM to someone you don't know is when you send a friend request. In this case, it's a good idea to send a short, respectful note that explains why you want to connect, as discussed in Chapter 2.

CHAPTER 6

LANGUAGE

This chapter provides language resources for using Faceþook.

Birthdays

Most people enjoy receiving good wishes on their birthday. Facebook will tell you when your friends' birthdays are (if they have permitted it). Just click on their name, and if you are allowed to write something on their wall, a brief message is fine (just *Happy birthday*, for example). You can also add a short phrase, like this:

- *Happy birthday! Hope it's wonderful.*
- *Happy birthday! Have a great day.*

You don't need to add special stickers or gifs or photos, although you can add those—especially if you know the person well. However, if I get an enormous image of a bunch of red roses that sparkle, from someone I don't know, it feels a little odd. If I don't know you well, *Happy birthday, Dorothy* is just fine.

If you click the person's name and find that you cannot post on that person's wall, then do not send the person a personal message (unless you know them very, very well). That person is trying to indicate that they do not want a lot of messages like that. Respect their wishes.

If your friend speaks a different language, you can google for how to say "happy birthday" in that language, or you can simply say it in English (assuming that is your common language) or your own language.

Holidays

Most holiday greetings use the word "happy," such as

- *Happy New Year!*
- *Happy Ramadan!*
- *Happy Independence Day!*
- *Happy Hanukkah!*

One common exception is Christmas:

- *Merry Christmas!*

You can also check to see what kinds of greetings or messages other people are posting.

Weddings and Anniversaries

You can simply say Congratulations! or expand it to an expression like one of these:

- *Congratulations to both of you!*
- *Congratulations on your engagement / marriage!*
- *Congratulations! I'm sure you'll both be very happy.*
- *Wishing you many years of happiness.*
- *Thirty years! Wow! That's wonderful!*

Good news

When a friend posts good news—finishing a Ph.D. program or becoming an aunt or uncle or completing a marathon or getting a new job—it's nice to post a brief message of congratulations. Use patterns like these:

- *Wonderful news!*
- *That's great! I'm very happy for you.*
- *Glad to hear that.*
- *Congratulations! You deserve it.*

You can also 'like' the post, even if you don't add a separate message. This shows the person that you read the news and wish them well.

Sometimes you might see close friends joking with the person about the good news, posting comments that might seem sarcastic or a little rude. Very close friends can joke like this in English; but if you are not very close, such a joke might be misinterpreted. You are always safe posting genuine good wishes, though, and that's what I recommend.

If you see many people responding to the news, understand that your friend might not have time to personally answer each message of congratulations.

Bad news

Understandably, people have a harder time responding to bad news. You don't want to say the wrong thing.

However, if someone has chosen to post about their bad news on Facebook, it's because they want to inform people, and probably also because they want some emotional support. You don't need to post something very long or detailed; even a short response lets the person know you saw the message and wish them well. Use a phrase like one of these:

- *I'm very sorry to hear that.*
- *Sorry for your loss.*
- *Deepest condolences, Carlos.*
- *I'm so sorry, Yuko.*
- *Wishing you the best at this difficult time.*
- *I don't have any advice, but my thoughts are with you.*

Note: Unless you know that you share the person's religion, do *not* offer expressions from your own religion.

USEFUL VOCABULARY

Some of these are new words; others are new meanings or new ways of using old words.

app: Short for application, this means some kind of software program. Apps that send you invites on Facebook, such as quizzes or games, are generally collecting personal information about you for marketing purposes.

event: It's possible on Facebook to invite people to an offline event (a birthday party or a dinner, for example) or an online event (a live chat or webinar, for example). If someone invites you to an event, Facebook will ask you to say if you are *going*, *not going*, or *interested*, and then will remind you when the event is coming up

follow / unfollow: You can follow someone on Facebook without becoming their friend. You'll see their public newsfeed. If you are already friends with someone, however, you can choose to unfollow them. Then you will stay friends, but their posts won't appear in your newsfeed.

friend / unfriend: Here's a noun that has also become a verb: *How many friends do you have? / I friended my roommate from college. / I unfriended my cousin because we had a fight.*

invite: Traditionally used just as a verb (*I'd like to invite you to join my closed group*), this is now used as a noun as well, to mean the same thing as *invitation*: *Please send me an invite to your secret group.*

like: Another verb that has become a noun in Facebook-land: *Did you see how many likes your photo got?*

newsfeed: The list of posts that appears on your page. It will be a mix of things your friends posted, posts from groups you're a member of, and paid advertisements.

notification: The announcements that Facebook sends you when something happens. You can control what kind of notifications you get (likes? comments? personal messages?) as well as how you get them (as emails? not at all?). The verb is **notify**. *Sorry I didn't know it was your birthday! I missed the notification / Facebook didn't notify me!*

OP: Original Poster. This means the person who started the thread, or conversation. *The OP wasn't asking for a recipe, she was asking for a restaurant recommendation.*

post: Both a noun and a verb. *Did you see her post about the election?* Or, *I don't post on weekends. I turn the computer off, and spend time with my family.*

share: Usually a verb (*Feel free to share this story*), but sometimes a noun: *My post about how to stop wasting water got 89 likes and 5 shares.*

snooze: To stop notifications from one person for a limited amount of time (usually 30 days). *I had to snooze Kim. All she talks about these days is her new dog!*

sponsored story: You'll see this in small letters above some posts in your newsfeed. This means someone has paid for that information to be shown. It's a kind of advertisement, in other words.

tag: Both a noun and a verb. Verb: *Can you tag Hiroko? She's the person standing on the left.* Noun: *Hi, Ahmed. Would you mind* *removing the tag of me on that photo? I don't want it to show up in my newsfeed.*

thread: One conversation. An OP (original poster) starts the thread, and then other people comment. Sometimes a person will *hijack the thread*, or change the subject.

AFTERWORD

Perhaps the best way to be a successful user of Facebook is to monitor your own feelings as you use it.

- What kinds of posts are interesting to you?
- What kinds of posts are useful, and why?
- What makes you happy?
- What annoys you?
- Who (and what kind of person) do you like to follow or interact with?

The culture of communication on Facebook is constantly evolving. And now that you're participating, you have the power to add to that evolution. Be interesting, be engaging, be kind... and be yourself.

See you online!

www.ingramcontent.com/pod-product-compliance
Lightning Source LLC
LaVergne TN
LVHW052314060326
832902LV00021B/3880